Círculo Rojo

The centre of our Universe:
We all are!

THE CENTRE OF OUR UNIVERSE:

WE ALL ARE!

PEDRO CAMARERO PRIETO

Círculo Rojo
EDITORIAL

Primera edición: noviembre 2020

Depósito legal: AL 2039-2020

ISBN: 978-84-1374-383-7

Impresión y encuadernación: Editorial Círculo Rojo

© Del texto: Pedro Camarero Prieto
© Maquetación y diseño: Equipo de Editorial Círculo Rojo
© Fotografía de cubierta: Depositphotos.com

Editorial Círculo Rojo
www.editorialcirculorojo.com
info@editorialcirculorojo.com

Impreso en España — Printed in Spain

The centre of our Universe

(We all are!)

I do not mind being alone in my present confinement. I feel I can communicate with everything that surrounds me and empathize with it. But what I find most compelling is the need to talk to someone that hopefully uses a similar language to mine. Someone who also perceives the world around me in a similar way. What would I give to see a pair of eyes that could reflect even just a little understanding!.

I reflected for a while longing for a human that could fit this description. I tried to recall from the depth of my memory the faces of those whose sensibilities and sensitivities were akin to mine. Quite a few gravitated towards my mind but, even though they evoked gratifying feelings, I somehow found them lacking the expertise that I would certainly need in that marvelous adventure I wanted to embark myself on. Then, as I squinted my eyes gazing at the smoldering sunset afar, a tenuous outline of a ship began to emerge against the darkish redness that was beginning to envelope me.

I sensed my mood was changing and I began to feel nostalgic. It rolled back a few decades of the human calendar and transported me to a courtyard in London where I could see myself sitting under the relaxing protection of a fatherly cherry tree. There I had once said goodbye, amid some tears and boundless gratitude, to an entity that had provided me with some of the tools that had helped me see the world in a light that I would never have been able to do on my own alone. And that time he had departed in a ship too. I could still picture his image at the helm waving his laurel garland as a symbolic advice. I started to feel emotional and my eyes began to blur. I closed them and let myself go.

After a relatively short while Achilles eased himself into the forefront of my memories and began to softly recite that old poem that had served to summarize nearly all my endeavors when, during our first encounter, I asked him to guide me through the perilous landscapes of infinity. Definitely it was him again to my rescue. Nobody could have remembered the words so well.

Islet in a shapeless sea of doubts,
Thou offer shelter to the stricken ship.
Hope that mine in its eternal sailings
Into your harbour may glide.

No reasoning can locate your place,
Kingdom of Neptune? … perhaps,
Imaginary sighting of land? … perhaps,
Longitude nought. Latitude infinite. No space.

On I sail glad to ignore where you reside,
Veering North, and South, and East, and West,
Engraving –unknowingly—on the sea surface your face.

Yet, when Aeolus neglects my sails, alas your features will fade.
Overboard this bottled message must go now,
Uncork it if you find it and let its essence out.

- "Lovely to see you again, Achilles, you are looking so well!", --I greeted him uttering these words with a mixture of excitement and affection. "I think I ought to tell you have always been present in my life ever since the day you regarded me fit enough to run the race of life 'on my own two legs', as you would probably phrase ", I said smiling gratefully.

Smiling back he said: "I know you have been following my coaching methods as much as possible in this new habitat of yours. I would also dare to hazard that perhaps it has not been as much as you would have liked. But I can understand that. Circumstances are not always conducive to exploring and learning with a similar degree of success. They always condition the outcome. And I would probably not be mistaken if I said that I can detect some kind of weariness in your stance, not to mention your voice. You have quite clearly been subjected to some passing of time. And, unlike me, you are obviously showing your fortunate human dimension."

The tone with which he said his last sentence left me somewhat baffled. Had I sensed some kind of emotion only akin to humans?. Could he really be showing the possible burden of eternal existence?. I decided to make a mental note of it as something worth exploring some other time.

 He stopped my musing and asked me: " Why did you call me back this time?. Another interesting trip into some unexplored lands?" He looked at me with some expectation.

-"Well, --I began --what I am about to propose to you this time is not so much a journey but a theoretical incursion into the plight of man in the universe, and a plausible analysis of it. And I would like you to start helping me even with my first steps because I am doubtful as to where to begin".

Achilles seemed to reflect a little before uttering his response: "Your proposition sounds appealing enough to me. But just before we set off together let me point out that our analysis will be just one out of the many that could be done. And also one of many that could sound sensible enough. Of course that will be something for each man to assess and judge. Now let's proceed to your first question, the starting point: I can see no better way to start than by placing man **AT THE CENTRE OF HIS UNIVERSE**".

 - "Centre of his universe?. I asked".

- "Well, my theory revolves around certain key concepts. They will reveal themselves as we go along. The first one that comes into view as regards the task ahead is the need to place man at the centre of his own universe. We both agreed long ago that the only way we could conceive how the universe might be was for it to be infinite. Remember how hard we tried to imagine it with limits and how we always failed to do so. There was always more space behind the hypothetical boundaries. So we concluded that one of the inescapable characteristics of the universe was its infinity. And that is very relevant for man as a societal being".

- "In what sense could that be relevant for man as a social being?", I enquired.

 - "In the sense that that would allow men to visualize themselves, each one of them as being the centre of their own universe, with all that it entails in terms of **not being discriminatory**. You, me, your neighbour, and so on, in universal terms are the centre of it. Nobody would be more relevant than the rest. Nobody would be more central or important than anybody else. In that sense we are all the middle point of our own universe, the point where everything around us converges and makes us what we are."

He stopped himself after sensing my interest in making a comment.

"At first sight I would not object to that idea" I replied. "Firstly because I certainly cannot disprove that we are all at the centre of a limitless universe. In other words if we knew its limits we could also pinpoint its centre somewhat. And secondly I'm beginning to like also the fact that that idea conveys a greater degree of equality . In fact in principle it would make us all relatively equal. A sort of the balanced and natural Justice one would expect from our Maker, the Universe."

Here I paused for a bit. Then continued.

 - "On the other hand, and somehow in contrast to the previous apparent appeal of everybody enjoying the same preeminence in space , when we level the charge of "egocentric" at someone it always seems to carry some damning connotations of their behaviour.   This according to your view would be something that could be said of everybody and without having necessarily to imply anything untoward, right?."

Achilles nodded. Then added: " Being egocentric is an inescapable characteristic of men. What happens is that most times we tend to confuse the concept of egocentricity with that of egoism or selfishness in their most basic and primitive sense. And while the degree of egocentricity is something we can do nothing about, in other words we can't be any other way, the degree of selfishness or egoism is something **we can** vary. It is in our hands, or rather in our brain, where our consciousness resides, that the ability to spread it around, so thin as to make it appear altruism, lies.

How we develop that ability has to do with being aware of what surrounds us. How big and precise the knowledge of our surroundings is will determine how much we can dilute the density of our intrinsic and **natural selfishness**. For selfishness is also a natural **mechanism for survival**. Only that as we mature it inevitably keeps striking different balances in accordance with the developing pace of our consciousness.

And now that we have used words such as awareness, knowledge and consciousness it would not come amiss to ask ourselves how we go about acquiring knowledge."

He stopped and stared at me. I got some flashbacks from the time I first met Achilles. How amazed I was at his ability to take every idea in his stride and also at the way he showed me how easily they all linked with one another in ever-changing shapes. I also remembered how often I had to ask him to shorten "*his stride*" so that I could keep pace with him.

- "Yes. How do you think we go about obtaining knowledge?. What is the way in which we humans start constructing our reality?." I asked.

- "We do it through our senses. Already in the womb even before we are born we begin gathering data that will be useful to maximizing our chances for survival. The process takes place in waves of concentric circles*, much in the same way that a stone creates waves as it hits the surface of a pond. Let's remind ourselves here of the egocentricity question we talked about before, and also of selfishness as a survival mechanism. Babies in their smallest circle will only recognise their mother as key to their wellbeing, and their **unrestrained selfishness** will play an essential role in getting what they want irrespective of their mother's needs. As time passes and they grow up -- and this is always done slightly differently by all of them -- they will start to realize that their satisfaction is not met with the same lightning speed as before. Their mother has become aware of the fact that she can attend to some of her needs a bit more before she devotes herself to her baby's. And so in the babies, in step with their mothers' actions, the process of diluting their unadulterated selfishness starts. Where there was only one entity at birth to think about, now there appears to be another person whose needs they have to make allowances for if they want to be treated in the most satisfactory manner. That means that their needs and her needs have to be taken into account together for them to have the best possible attention from her. Thus in fact their selfishness has been slightly diminished for they no longer think solely of their own needs but also of the needs of another. This interestingly enough will turn out to be **for their benefit** in the long run.

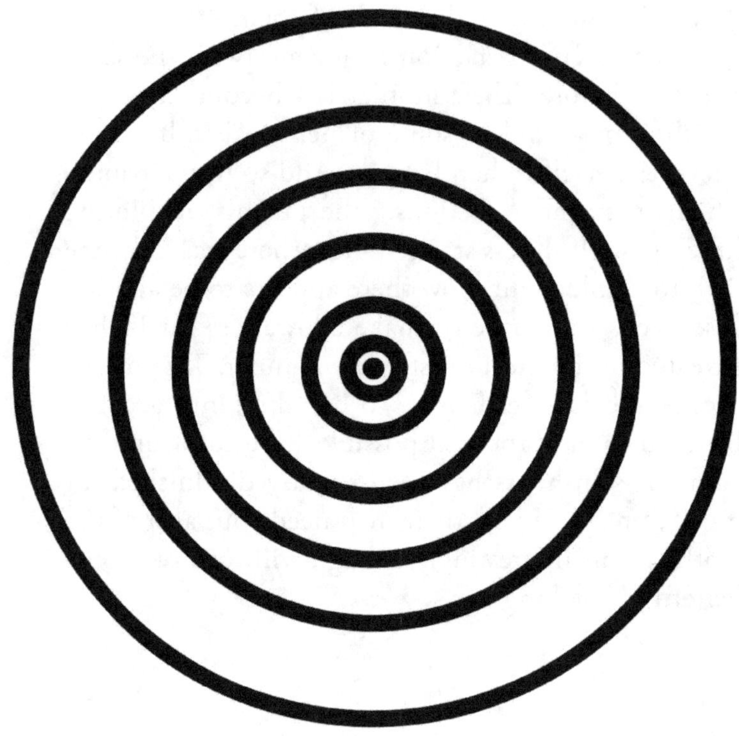

*In reality these circles are not distinct and separate from one another. They are not part of any discrete set. They are all part of a continuum in space. The image is only here to help us visualize in a broad sense how it works.

Later other members of the children´s families will interact with them in wider circles. Each one of them with their own movements and different speeds will try to fulfill their essential needs. With those movements and needs, everybody going in and out of each other's space, they will perceive **learning** about one another's speeds and necessities **as beneficial** in order to avoid all sorts of collisions, which would be damaging for them all. And in the meantime while this is all happening the children will be observing the motions of those bodies around them and will also

internalize that it is better to **KNOW** how they move, and what their needs might be, so that they also avoid colliding with them.

Then as we broaden the circles and get out of our home into wider spaces we will enter into contact with other living creatures. Our little and particular universes, (those concentric circles of limited knowledge), all of them with slightly varying characteristics, will crisscross one another in our daily activities with the risk of possible conflicts. Then we could expand the circles to include not only our home, and our street, but also our neighborhood, district, town, region, nation, and on and on. Consequently, **each circle** carries with it its inherent need for **new knowledge**.

Perhaps now we can more readily visualize how **knowing** the way others move around and what their needs might be could be essential for our traversing their particular universes without crashing head on into them, or even having some major grazing. Minor grazings will hardly ever be avoidable given the **different degrees of awareness** of those involved, and the impossibility for human beings of attaining absolute knowledge.

Not as easy as it appears to be, you might think. But I would argue in favor of trying to look inwards at yourself, at what you are and what your **essential needs** are. And after having done that you will most probably come to realize that the rest of the human species are very much like you, and their basic needs are the same as yours with hardly any really relevant differences. Therefore before we take a course of action, that obviously is going to fulfill some of our needs, we ought to analyze whether that benefit that we have foreseen is in some way harmful to those whose little universe is going to cross ours at some time or another. Because if it is damaging to them it means it will sooner or later be damaging to us. **They** have to be taken into account as being **also recipients** of the benefits that our actions will bring about.

In that way that somewhat shortsighted selfishness, which lies at one end of that yardstick we use to measure this behaviour with, will start moving gradually towards the other end which is where **altruism** resides. Remember: **we are all interconnected**.

The sooner we understand that the big Universe is a sum of all those interrelated little universes [1] moving constantly around at different speeds, -- each carrying their particular needs --, the more harmonious our journey will be, which in turn will result in much less unnecessary distress."

Achilles paused for a while and I took my turn.

" I agree with you when you say that knowing yourself will be equated to knowing everybody, if what you mean is that we all use the **SAME PROCESS** of **REASONING** and that the only thing that makes us different is **WHAT** we process, that is to say the information gathered through our senses, which is to some degree common and to some degree particular to all of us."

Once more I felt deeply attached to him, he had come to my aid as he had always done when called upon. He had given me the push I needed to get started. That degree of likeness that had struck me during our first escapade into the dizzying notion of infinity grabbed me again. He had, at that time, become the Archetypal character of the human species, and his mythical contest with the tortoise had come to symbolize the perennial struggle of men in their attempt to understand reality by means of logic and reason. Forever trying and forever failing. Filling with **drama and poetry** the play of human existence on the universal stage.

---

1   In these "universes" we should include all living things, even though some of them may lack "apparent" mobility at first sight. And some would also argue that all types of inanimate matter in the Universe should also be included.

He realized that perhaps it was not a bad moment to leave me on my own, to do what I had thought I should do before my personal running neared its end. So after confiding that he had had some requests from other places in the world, where the reenactment of his mythical race was still appreciated as a matter of debate, he waved me goodbye from his boat, and pointed to his laurels as if wishing me to remember **how to win**. Gradually he sailed off into the distance.

I knew his leaving me was not really true. I sensed he would always be around somehow. As I breathed deeply I stared at the comforting and relaxing motion of the waves. My thoughts started to gather. After a while they resolved themselves into a definite feeling: I had to try and write a reasonable account of my personal race against the tortoise. A race whose final outcome I definitely knew, but which would not deprive me from trying to find out how close to my goal I would get.

How our mind works. The process of Reasoning

Having placed man at the centre of his universe it could perhaps be useful now to try and explain that theory Achilles had told me about, regarding the mechanics of our rational mind.

The lengthy conversations we had on the subject still echo in my head. I remember how reasonably satisfied we remained after we had worked out an image that would eventually end up symbolizing the way our mind, our mental spaceship, traveled through the universe. A universe that was **ever-changing!**. And **that** was another property, apart from its infinity, to be added to our universe: **CONSTANT CHANGE**. A universe in which everything : shapes, speeds, flows, densities, all types of matter, visible or otherwise, was in perennial flux.

Not only did we work out the design of our mental spaceship but we also decided, thanks mainly to Achilles's expertise on the field, what philosophical fuel would be most beneficial for men to negotiate a landscape in perennial motion and its infinity. That philosophical fuel would be **IDEALISM**.

I remember us thinking that Idealism, whose main tenet is "**Esse est percipi**" would be that philosophical system that could perhaps symbolize best the way our human reasoning strove to make sense of an incessant and infinite universe, trying to move in harmony with that eternal cosmic dance.

And much in a similar way to how we saw that the thought of us being the centre of our universe gave rise to a feeling of equality, Idealism would also add its own non-discriminatory load to the idea of us all being rather alike, because in contrast to the doctrines that would argue in favor of an indispensable outside factor, Idealism would place solely within our mind the creation of **our** world[2]. This thought would enjoy in principle a greater feeling of equality than the idea that an external factor could condition the global concept of Reality, since with the latter, there would always be the risk that some *"enlightened visionaries"* could self-proclaim themselves as being closer than everybody else to that **extrinsic** component of our Reality.

We assume, as the Idealists do, that the way we perceive reality is the way reality[3] is, that's to say a **construct of the mind**. Our five senses, limited though they are, have been developed to help us adapt and survive in our environment. And it is through the five known senses that we build up our reality. A reality that will be **common**[4], and **different** too, to a degree to all of us. The reasoning process would be the same for the human species, the only thing varying in it being the input, or information, gathered by our senses from our surroundings, be them physical or cultural.

---

2   When we perceive a table, or anything else for that matter, we establish a unique relationship with whatever is the object of our perceptions. But if we stop perceiving it, it does not mean that the table disappears and ceases to exist. What does disappear is our individual relationship with it. The table, however, will continue its existence for those observers that perceive it and establish their own relationship with it.

3   We would add here that that perceived reality is both dependent upon its own inherent change and upon the evolution of the observer. And though its inherent change may be imperceptible, therefore irrelevant, what we think we "see" one day will become a new reality as a result of our changing. That change is particularly noticeable whenever some new piece of knowledge is acquired.

4   It is upon this common ground that our society has built its structures. A common ground shared by supposedly all its members.

Some Idealists mention that we also have a sixth sense that may have been developed as a direct consequence of the limited scope of the other five to solve the ever more complex questions that arose as we created our civilizations : our **IMAGINATION**. Our imagination helps us transcend our physical perceptions and get closer to otherwise inaccessible realities. But all of this has to be done **within REASON**, through the sensible tools that mother nature has provided us with.

 And how do we use our **REASONING POWERS?**. Let's have a look at that mental spaceship in which we travel through the universe and which takes the shape of a bubble. That is if you look at it from the front or the back. But if you do it sideways you shall also see within the bubble the clear outline of a maneuverable cone.

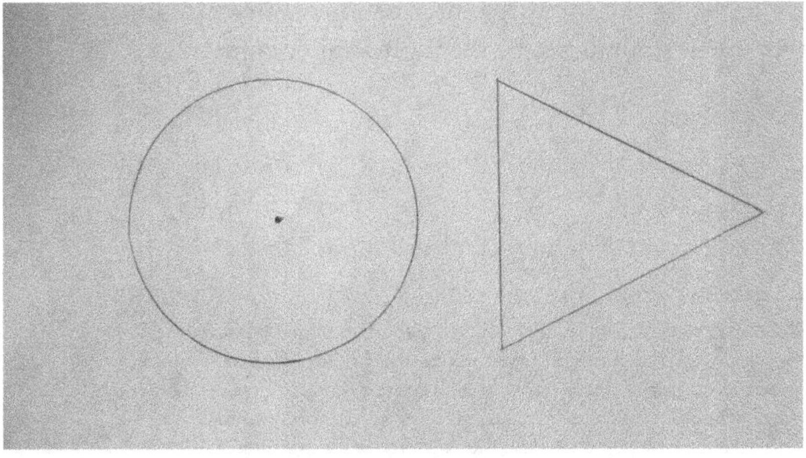

A basic view of the design of our mental spacecraft

Human Reasoning is essentially very simple. It's all about comparing things we perceive. We compare two objects, two sensations, two feelings, two whatever, and then through our analysis we detect differences and similarities, and after that we start defining, classifying and categorizing. Then the process carries on adding a new element and doing the same analysis, and so on. The differences would equate with the **Particular** world and the similarities with the **Universal**, the all encompassing view we need to have so much. Be it called, God, Nature, the Universe and so on.

But how would the cone image help us to visualize our attempt to decipher the universe?. It could be said that at the vertex of the cone man would be seen at its command centre, piloting his mental craft as he explores and tries to make sense of the chaos in that particular universe that surrounds him, whereas the base of the cone would represent that inescapable need man has to find an all-embracing and coherent vision, be it religious or philosophical, of the particular factors experienced. That vision would afford him a semblance of general Order. So the **vertex** would point towards **Particularism**, and the base towards **Monism**. Each particular experience lived through by man would have to be understood and made to fit at the base within the existing global conception of his universe. Even if that meant moving, reshaping and expanding the old Order.

We could also figure out some of the properties of the material our bubble-ship had been made of. It would have to be **permeable, pliable** and **expandable**. These qualities would allow its cone-like shape to adapt to every movement of the man inside, with the consequent positional variations of the vertex and the base.

 It would also have to be **translucent** rather than transparent. Achilles had taught me, in the epic dramatization of his race against the tortoise, by the Greek philosopher Zeno of Elea, that transparency would open the gateway to the corruptive influence of the concept of infinity with all its maddening multiplications and subdivisions of space. Such vision would not be conducive to reasoning, as the great Argentinian writer *Jorge Luis Borges* brilliantly depicts in the short story "*Funes el memorioso*", where an apparently immeasurable process of subdivisions of space takes place, and Funes, after suffering an accident, is portrayed as having gone infinitely beyond the present capabilities of human perceptions in an all-out attempt to conquer reality through his senses. Unable to reason because of the relentless influx of perceptions, which would not allow him time for a "*reasonable breather*", he is said to have met with an early death due to lung congestion. He had died pursuing, literally to *his exhaustion*, that slippery and indescribable dog of his, in the same manner that Achilles would eternally be pursuing his elusive tortoise.

In such a protective bubble we go through life making our decisions. Decisions that will be in accordance with the Monistic view which lies at the base of the cone. That monistic view at the base will be made up mainly of all the principles that our society has provided us with, through either social interaction, education, mass media, or other social agents, and perhaps with the addition of other ones incorporated by ourselves after reflecting about some particular experiences we have had, whose explanations escaped the accepted framework. What we usually mean as **reality** in social terms would be that portion of the base of our cone that is **common** to all of us. Naturally enough there will always be some parts in our monistic view which will differ.

Man could be seen as being placed in an indefinite universe, poised between two tendencies: one heading towards **particularity** and the other towards **universality**. And, as mentioned previously, our individual task would be that of trying to instill some sense into the apparent disorder of our particular world. Each particular factor we can identify will of necessity be compared and analyzed to set off its similarities and its differences. Then it will be cataloged and categorized accordingly, and placed at the base in its corresponding and orderly place. By doing that we will have increased the knowledge of our world a little bit.

Traveling inside that apparently streamlined spaceship, the vertex spearheading it, and keeping both the vertex and the base within reasonable reach we are relatively safe. As we said the material of which the bubble is made up allows for the theoretical cone to be imagined as every time we enter into contact with something there will always be a certain point in the bubble that has come into contact sooner and more intensely than the others.

We will be forever running up and down our mental cone **pushing at both ends**. And whenever the particular end of our world presents us with a new experience, that is to say something not codified previously, which has filtered through into our idealist bubble, we shall have to subject it to our rational approach, and that new bit of awareness acquired will have to be accommodated at the base of our cone updating our monistic view accordingly. So we can be sure that in a universe that is in perennial flux our process of reasoning will never come to an end, and our Achilles will always enjoy new challenges in which to show his poetic and dramatic stride.

Movement: The essence of life. The fuel of reason.

Without having to look back at what we have written so far we would not run a great risk if we said that of all the words used those denoting some degree of movement would most likely rank as the most numerous. The reason being that **movement** appears to be **THE** ever present feature in the universe.

Especially within the Particular world, which is the one that will concern our species by and large. And notably also because just as it was previously said that infinity was an inevitable conclusion when reflecting on the possible limits, or not, of the universe, in the same manner we also seem to be unable to have a Monistic view of it, due to our incapability to place ourselves somewhere outside its boundaries. If we have admitted the absence of limits, we will have to accept that stepping outside them is not a conceivable proposal.

Up to the present day it looks like that the problem of the origins of life is still an open-ended question whose answer may lie shrouded *ad aeternum* in the misty realms of infinity, inaccessible to our limited human powers of reasoning. Perhaps as we journey through the universe, inside our naturally evolved idealist bubble, with our rational efforts pushing its boundaries further and further back, in an attempt to encompass an ever greater expanse, we may one day see ourselves on the threshold of the divine abode, perhaps sensing we are a bit closer to finding out if there was really an actually "**discernible beginning**" at all [5]. And

---

5   We also assume here that the concept of nothingness is inconceivable, which in turn would lead us to think that the **inevitable interconnection** that links everything in the universe would probably have to play a **key role** in the insoluble

yet, even then the crossing of the threshold would of necessity be another endless odyssey without the possibility of locating some time-space coordinates as an answer to that question. But, ... if it were to happen that in the eternal flow of time one day we ended up entering that abode we would all have ceased to be ourselves and would have become **One**. Then, as a result, we would KNOW everything!. Life. Its origins. Everything there is to know. We would have reached omniscience, total knowledge. We would be in step with the eternal cosmic dance.

But acquiring absolute awareness was unfortunately an impossibility.

An unfortunate impossibility?. Was it really *"unfortunate"*?.

Could it also not be felt the other way around?. Being an impossibility might also be regarded as rather fortunate perhaps for both man and the Universe itself. (I will let the readers work out that one by themselves).

However, thinking along the lines of the Idealist philosophy where the role of the **perceiver**, or **observer**[6], is crucial to existence, it could very well be proposed that movement, that is to say the infinite and ceaseless forces interacting in the universe, would have engendered our mind. It was as if the universe had somehow felt the compelling desire to know itself through the particular, or to have something bear witness to his own performance, to achieve self awareness, and only by creating our little mind would it be able to fulfill such desire.

---

problem of identifying the origin of life with a defined time and place. Perhaps it is more reasonable, even more aesthetic, to think that the notion of life - some kind of consciousness - permeates everything in the universe. If so, we could end up visualizing **infinite states and levels of awareness.**

6   Interesting to notice the similarities that can be drawn between Idealism and Quantum Mechanics.

One question that could possibly arise now is whether that desire would be able to enjoy total fulfillment. In other words could the universe have a longing for absolute knowledge acquired via its own creatures?. It would be reasonable to assume that the complete realization of that fulfillment would bring about a kind of ecstatic immobility. Achilles would have caught up with the tortoise and gained total knowledge. They both would have become One. Movement would have ceased for him. (Only the little, particular, minds can experience movement or change).

Somehow it might appear reasonable to think that movement in the universe would have created our mind. And what would be somewhat paradoxical is the fact that, through our rational process, we would apparently have the elimination of movement as a final goal, that is to say we would want to do away with what gave rise precisely to our mind. So, the universe apart from having the wish of wanting its creatures to get to know it it also has a built-in ploy whereby that wish can never be realized. **Enter infinity**, and with it the wish's inherent impossibility of attainment.

We believe that there has been movement forever and it appears reasonable to think there always will be. And we will hazard to say that movement will preserve itself eternally, and will do so possibly thanks to its inherent desire for immobility. Such an insatiable desire for an unattainable state would not be an end in itself, but a means to the very end: infinite movement.

Having propounded that movement in its varying differences and degrees had been the creator of our mind we will now try to focus our reflections on the idea that the **perception of movement** is also the natural fuel that keeps our rational engine running. Something that appears logical enough, but that also deserves some careful considerations as regards the degree of clarity and ceaseless proliferation, or otherwise, of such perceptions.

It could be said that for man's reasoning to function at an **optimum state** such reasoning should take place within certain flexible parameters of his perceptions. Those limits, here again, being specific to every individual, would be those that would allow him to have both tendencies, Pluralism and Monism, the Particular and the Universal, **within sensible reach**. Because it would not be conducive to reasoning to not see the forest because of the trees, or, conversely, not to see the trees because of too large a perspective. For our reasoning race to be felt in good condition it would have to keep both extremes of our bubble cone within manageable distances, always able to find the paths that link both our particular world and our all-embracing global Order.

It would be along those paths, linking the particular with the universal, where the actual reasoning takes place, those basic mental activities of comparing, of finding differences and similarities, of classifying and of categorizing would need to be done to extract some understanding of our experiences and increase our awareness.

And what happens to our mind when our reasoning process is deprived of a **balanced input of movement**, such as being subjected to either an incessant proliferation of perceptions, or conversely, when it is subjected to a noticeable privation of them?.

By an unfortunate coincidence these days quite a large proportion of human beings are being subjected to the latter situation, that is to say they are being compelled to endure a severe privation of a healthy dose of changes in the perceptions of their particular world. Having to stay at home within surroundings that are all too familiar, which have been *reasoned through* for so long, which hardly offer any possibility for something new to occur, is a stifling environment for the process of reasoning to survive in. Our reason has evolved thanks to the **perception of changes** and the consequent need to make sense of them. So in order to keep a **healthy equilibrium** in our mind, and make it thrive, we need to have a diet that provides a certain amount of particular factors to our universe, each with its varying degrees of novelty nutrients. The result of this being absent, that is to say of not perceiving enough movement, is an overwhelming feeling of **apathy and boredom**.

But boredom may not be the only feeling arising from confinement in a relatively small space. At the same time that the process of knowledge acquisition of our material surroundings starts at birth, another essential process also begins: that of getting to be aware, not only of the physical world, but also of ourselves as **members of the same species**. And here comes again the same essential tool that defines us: *reasoning*.

The most basic reasoning process as regards finding what we are also takes place in our innermost circle around us, the one that encompasses not just "**me**" but also "**you**". So we first start realizing who we are by contrasting our movements with those of our mother. Then as we broaden our circles other human entities will become "him", "her", "yous" and finally "them". Every time we contrast our movements with those of other people we reinforce our personality as individuals. So having a sensible number of people to compare ourselves against makes for a **healthy psychological balance**. In fact, it could be said that we are who we are thanks to all those that have entered our universe. Everybody in a way is like a mirror of slightly varying compositions that reflect back the light that we project onto them, thus allowing us to see different aspects of our own make-up.

So, for rational beings like us, who derive an important part of our psychological balance from contrasting what we are with others, to be in a situation of confinement means having far fewer people nearby to contrast with, which results in the fact that the daily dose of "*healthy*" contrasting activity that is usually shared among many other people in our social interactions will have to be administered to only a few individuals, or maybe just one, which is when that contrasting, when doing it **too often** with **the same recipients**, may transform into confronting, and this in turn into different levels of conflict, which as we all know can result in harmful behaviour. Thus apparently the upsurge in family violence that is taking place during the lockdown.

On the other hand we have also had plenty of social representations of our other psychological need, which naturally has its roots at the base of our mental spaceship. As we know at the base of the cone lies our monistic view of the universe, where everything that we experience has to fit into an all-embracing idea that will give us that sense of Order that we need, be it termed as *God, Nature, the Universe*, and so on. All those massive displays of solidarity that can be observed are evidence of our need to transcend ourselves, our particular worlds, and feel that we are all really bound into **One**.

It is worth noticing that the concept that symbolizes this need in man usually surfaces most irrepressibly when he is suddenly confronted with the transient nature of life and the reality of losing loved ones becomes too hard to bear. It is in this situation that we come up with the idea of an **imperishable and omniscient Being** that will turn chaos into a sort of immutable or harmonious Order in which everything and everybody will find their rightful and permanent place.

 Will we ever be able to learn and **internalize** that each and every decision that we make transcends our particular universe and affects **the Whole?**. Or will that always remain within the precinct of just a few wise men, lucky enough to have seen the interconnectedness of the particular world, and also to have realized that human happiness could not be pursued outside themselves, in the material world, but **lay within their mind**?. Have a guess yourselves dear readers.

In the meantime we could perhaps try to find also some behavioral representation in our more normal social routines, --that is to say not related to these months' lockdown, -- of how much we are conditioned by our perceptions, both in their abnormal proliferation or their undue privation. And talking about social routines and their corresponding linguistic clichés we cannot have failed to hear innumerable times that sentence that summarizes very concisely the fact that we have been exposed to *a lot of new perceptions* for a certain period of time. When that feeling makes itself present what we really are longing for is that place that embodies like no other the monistic view of our little universe, where everything is known, where there are no uncertainties and where we feel very safe and at ease: "**There is no place like home**". Probably the first sentence uttered by most people as they cross the threshold of their home after some active holidays.

Conversely, when we have spent an excessive amount of time at home, --with each one of us having our own different **saturation point**,-- our mind starts itching for a change of environment. This is the kind of situation in which we find ourselves these days, in the times of the pandemic lockdown. Naturally enough the privileged ones that enjoy a larger space, where some amount of particular agents can find their way in, will definitely be able to endure their physical isolation with much less psychological stress. Those "*imprisoned*" within a very little space will run the risk of a mental breakdown because of their incapacity to reach the required balance in their mind. Perceiving some particular agents would provide that equilibrium and some sanity. And to illustrate linguistically this psychological phenomenon in English we have this age-old expression: "**A change is as good as a holiday**". When the feeling of boredom becomes overwhelming, when we sense that nothing "is happening" (movement is not being perceived), it is time for us to introduce a change into our life, to kickstart that reasoning process that had been stalled by the apparent absence of new perceptions.

There are also some ways in which just by contemplating nature we will probably detect the inextricable connection between movement and our most profound inner self. At times together with an intuitive realization of belonging. That inherent connection comes interwoven with that soothing sensation we feel when we simply stare vacantly at the waves on the beach, or when we gaze endlessly at the warming dancing of the flames in an open fireplace. Most human beings have experienced both situations and sensed their balmy influence on their minds. Not only due to their obvious manifestation of movement but most importantly their **frequency**, which apparently is just within the adequate parameters for us, neither too fast nor excessively slow.

Walking at a leisurely pace is also particularly conducive to reasoning. We have all read about how it was one of the preferred methods of teaching used by the great Aristotle. And even cycling at a very moderate speed can help us indulge in the pleasures of introspection.

There is no overstating the importance of knowing both the **nature** of our mental process and the **source of energy** that makes it tick. And as we have seen it is the perception of movement in all its infinitely varying ways. It is naturally obvious that there will be an instinctive response from our mind to try and correct any mental imbalance, provoked either by a flood of new perceptions o by a drought of them, but **being aware of how our mind works** will allow us to fine-tune its running and prevent us hopefully from reaching those extreme and harmful states.

In search of both: the Absolute and Total Knowledge.

We have previously touched just in passing over the subject of how our rational mind, being confronted with the apparently chaotic world that is always having to face, compounded with the awareness of our own ephemeral existence, may have started contemplating the idea of there perhaps being an entity that would not be affected by such human shortcomings.

And no other situation could have prepared our mind better for the **conception of the Absolute**   than the one we are going through at the moment, with this global pandemic that is undermining those seemingly solid foundations of our society.

As with the origins of life, the inception of the idea of the Absolute will probably lie hidden forever in the shifting pages of human history, but it would perhaps be not too unreasonable to propose that it would not be very far away from the times when we first started honoring our loved ones by placing them in a tomb. The act of building up necropolis was but an attempt to establish a somewhat **fixed** home in our ceaseless universe.

Such may have been our sense of powerlessness and hopelessness in those situations and so intense our longing for an eternal being that it may well have been brought into existence by such an irrepressible desire. Situations of extreme anguish are not the wholesome ecosystem that our rational process needs to survive in good health. The clear and distinct perceptions that it stems from, and needs to thrive on, are blurred into a rather vague and obscure mental landscape. It is amid this type of environment, full of uncertainty and uncontrollable fear, that the notion of the Absolute begins to loom large and fatherly. Eventually as the intensity of those feelings increase they will resolve themselves into the birth of the Absolute, an idea that will embody an entity which, unlike men, will not be subjected to any decay, it will be impervious to changes and eternal. These two attributes would naturally do away with the **concept of time.**

Here we could hypothesize a little about the idea of time. And for the sake of following the same lines of thought developed so far it would be useful for this purpose to familiarize ourselves a bit more with that supreme athlete we had the privilege of meeting at the beginning of this little piece of work: Achilles.

Zeno of Elea, a prominent disciple of Parmenides, in an attempt to find an irrefutable argument in support of the theory that movement was an illusory idea, created the ageless paradox of "Achilles and the Tortoise", in which a fleet-footed runner like Achilles would never catch up with the slow-moving tortoise. The crux of the paradox hinges upon the fact that Achilles gives the tortoise a head start. So by the time he reaches the position where the tortoise was the tortoise has already moved to a new point, then by the time he reaches that point, the tortoise has moved farther to another point, and on and on ad infinitum. Both eternally falling through ever more minute spaces, in pursuit of some sort of ecstasy emanating from that desired immobility.

This aesthetically appealing paradox, probably first used mainly to disprove the possibility of movement, could also in a way be used to dispense with time. For if we happened to consider that the idea of time was **secondary** to the perception of movement then it would necessarily follow that for time to exist movement has to be observed.

It is the awareness of both the decaying movement of our nature together with our transient existence which gives rise to the idea of the Absolute. Achilles (**man**) in his perennial pursuit of the tortoise (**reality**) will never be able to reach it. Man's rational approach, despite his endless efforts, will always fall short of getting to know reality. Our perceptions, however much they could be enhanced through our ingenuity, will never be able to apprehend the infinite degrees of movements that take place in the universe. This kind of situation causes curiously enough two different and complementary feelings in man. On the one hand **everlasting hopefulness** to perhaps one day be able to meet and be one with his creator, --cessation of movement and time, -- and on the other hand also **perpetual hopelessness** because of its inherent unattainability. The tortoise is rationally unreachable and reality is rationally unknowable.

The greater the degree of powerlessness or hopelessness, the greater our desire to acquire that state of immobility that reaching an absolute brings about. The absolute would, in fact, prevent our loved ones from leaving us, because even though they might appear to do so from our sensible dimension, nothing would escape from its gravitational field. And the more we believed in it, both in numbers and in fervor, the greater its influence on our particular worlds. That way those loved ones lost would revolve around it for a while until they found their proper and orderly place in an eventually fixed universe, where, we knew, they would stay forever. They would not be gone any more.

As it has been mentioned earlier it can reasonably be argued that finding, or having an Absolute would gradually cancel the perception of movement, freezing our universe as it continuously expanded and providing us also with an apparent **feeling of elation** at having found an infallible criterion to measure our world with. This realization will oblige us to make every human activity fit into the patterns of the Absolute with the consequent result of us constantly trying to superimpose its design over our universe. The specific weight of the Absolute, which would be forever on the increase as it expanded, would exert such a powerful attraction on our mind that we would be unable to escape from its influence. As we would keep on reasoning on our desire to vindicate its immutable nature our mental processes would be apparently gathering speed at the same time as they would be branching out in infinite directions solidifying everything we were able to perceive.

Fortunately though we believe that a rational vindication of the Absolute is **inconceivable**, since logically we would have an infinite number of Achilleses running after the same number of tortoises without ever catching up with them. We would have to give up reasoning in order to achieve immobility, the Absolute. After a vertiginous fall through the precipices of logic, our mind would not, at a certain point, be able to stand up to the pressure originated and would disintegrate. We would then have become irrational. Our only understanding of the universe would take place on an **instinctive level**. Our consciousness would have been lost.

That loss of awareness would mean not being able to detect changes. In fact in the end our universe would be fixed, immutable. No changes would also mean no time, and in this sense we could say that finding an Absolute would eventually translate into an immutable eternity. An eternity with no movement, frozen in time. Both concepts, the Absolute and Eternity with lack of movement could be considered **inconceivable and anti-rational**. Inconceivable, since we assume, as we have done so far, that the flow of the universe is perennial, and anti-rational because total stillness would do away not only with reason but with any other kind of life as we understand it today.

Having given rise to the notion of the Absolute to resolve our **unbearable existential distress** as a rational species, we humans, from a sociological standpoint, have also come up with another minor absolute which is aimed at putting some social order into the complex world of social dealings or exchanges. At the beginning it was gold, which as its divine counterpart would also enjoy some degree of incorruptibility and durability. Nowadays it is money. And the problem with all absolutes, be they major or minor, is that they have the inherent property of becoming **the measure of all things**, overshadowing, when not obliterating, many other, and most times more valid, criteria to judge our actions by. In fact one could easily argue that a great many of our troubles stem from that absurd and antinatural approach.

But let us proceed along now and try to focus on the notion of Total Knowledge, to see how it may compare to that of the Absolute.

Let us recapitulate a little the main ideas that our imaginary vision has been based upon. We have already argued that infinity had to be a necessary notion in our universal structure, because it was the only acceptable concept for a reasoning mind as far as space was concerned. Infinity would provide us with the pliable mental material we would need to mold the universe either in an **orderly or chaotic** conception, depending on which would suit our intellectual requirements. The concept of **order** would come about from that monistic view of the universe, and as such it could be regarded as immobile, since it is already everywhere, whereas the idea of **chaos** would stem from the introduction of the notion of particular factors and their untraceable movements within the monistic view.

And it is through those ceaseless movements within the monistic view that the universe ensures that we will not lose our vital sense of freedom, because we would not be able to work out the infinite causes that had determined our actions. That infinite chaos of the particular universe would serve to preserve not only our freedom but also that infinite hope so essential to us and to the universe itself, and which had been seemingly put at risk by the monistic view of the universe. For behind any conception of Order there lurk the menacing shadows of an extremely reasonable notion: **Absolute Determinism.**

We could hazard to say that determinism does make sense, but it is an infinite sense, something beyond our present capabilities for reasoning. It could perhaps be said that in the **universal equation** of man's determinism, the infinite number of circumstances converging upon him (the whole universe) would be the **unknown quantity** which would present the absolute impossibility of calculating the result of that equation. This impossibility would be commonly defined, with varying degrees of awareness, as our **free will.**

Having been subjected, with extreme intensity, to the insufferable influence of the transient nature of the particular world, men's mind generated the Absolute as an also natural response to assuage their anxiety. The Absolute would put a stop to the insidious movement . On the other hand, when conditions were not so oppressive as those described before, men would still have to negotiate the chaos of their particular world, the constant changes, in order to better their surroundings and improve their way of life. That, as it was pointed out at the beginning, means constantly enlarging our circles of knowledge, placing new observations under rational scrutiny and broadening each of us our monistic view of the universe. We have already seen that this process is a never-ending one. Man will never be able to acquire total knowledge. However close we may think we have got to knowing reality there will always be an unbridgeable gap between the tortoise and Achilles.

But if we, hypothetically, at a certain point in time, would manage to incorporate into our consciousness the infinite flows of the universe then we would have entered that theoretical timeless realm reserved for divine beings. We would not experience movement any more, **we would be in step with it**, therefore not sensing it. But unlike with the Absolute, where the resulting eternity would be irrationally static, with Total Knowledge movement would still exist, but with it not being perceived by us, having reached god-like status, who or what would perform the role of the spectator to witness it?. This could interestingly lead us to think that there might perhaps be some kind of **immanent awareness of itself in each different movement**, or for that matter in each particular constituent of the universe.

 We have by now realized that both finding an **Absolute** and acquiring **Total Knowledge** are basically anti-rational. Anti-rational because they would eventually prevent the process of reasoning once either of them was achieved. We have seen how the Absolute would stop all different movements by making them conform to its immutable essence in an infinitely freezing embrace. And we have also visualized how the attainment of omniscience would mean being in harmony, or moving in step, with all different flows in the universe. This God-like sensation would also dispose of the perception of movement, but would apparently allow for movement to still exist and be perceived by the particular elements within it. In a curious way it could be said that we, humans, through our reasoning process, --and the rest of the particular world to their own degree of awareness too,-- allow the Universe, Nature, or God to also feel the flow of time. In other words we might just be what could be called a **Divine pastime**.

Refocusing our priceless mind

And yet, running forever between both the particular and universal ends of our own mental spacecraft, the dramatic performance of human reasoning will always be taking place[7]. Each one of us will be applying our most stringent rational powers to try to squeeze the factor of **chance** out of our conclusions as much as possible. In that sense we should always be wary of applying too rigidly our previously gained knowledge, --useful, little, but imperfect absolutes,-- that helped us explain situations confronted earlier. Caution should always be the name of the game. Nothing is ever the same again. So we always have to make allowances for the new changes that may have taken place.

An ever-inquisitive mind will always be questioning the validity of any principle that leaves an unreasonably ample space to the unsettling influence of chance, to the unknown. And **thinking**, as it has already been pointed out, is not only being able to **overcome differences**, thus trying to reach a monistic Order (man pushing at the base of his spacecraft), but it is also being able to **break generalizations down**, to inquire into over-simplifying statements, thus trying to see the disparities within the particular disorder (man pushing at the vertex of his spacecraft). Whenever we feel that one of our little absolutes can provide a suitable answer to some particular thing we have observed we will not experience the need to probe any more into it. In fact our little

---

7   Apart from visualizing our special hero, Achilles, forever running up and down our cone-shaped bubble craft, it might also be helpful to liken our reasoning workings to the movement of a pendulum, swinging ceaselessly one way, then the other, from the Particular to the Universal, from Pluralism to Monism. And it could also be regarded as reasonable that when going through the middle point of the pendular swing our mind might find its optimum habitat for reasoning.

absolutes become the boundaries of our reasoning processes. And if that might be regarded as a plausible statement it may also be argued that some of us could very well be considered, too, as "*rationally dead*" while being physically still alive, because all our littles absolutes would provide us with all the answers we needed.

But for a reasoning man, who is aware also of the transient, and somewhat superstitious, nature of his own little absolutes, meaning that he is conscious of the fact that his reasonings are nothing but beliefs, those boundaries would just be something to be pushed constantly farther back, in an attempt to let an ever larger expanse of the universe be shed with rational light. And let us emphasize once more what the **wholesome dynamics** of our rational workings **consist of**: on the one hand it is fundamental not to lose sight of the individual, or particular world, because of too large a perspective, and on the other, also as important, not to let ourselves be unable to see the wood for the trees. Keeping within these guidelines and pushing energetically in both directions our rational well-being will be safely placed.

This apparently safe way of reasoning, provided by our idealist philosophy, that is to say keeping the essence of reality within our perceptive powers (which include our five senses; plus another one: imagination; plus the artificial tools we have developed to increase our perceptions) is not devoid of great universal drama though. And that sense of great drama would appear to start working the moment we realize that those powerful instruments we have invented to interpret the universe such as language and numbers, although undeniably vastly useful, trap us within their very creative **labyrinths**, eventually preventing us from reaching reality. In a universe that is in constant flux nothing can be knowable in absolute terms. However precise the reasoning picture may be, there will always be an indefinite degree of unperceived movement within it that will escape our rational take.

But being aware of the limitations of our reasoning process to gain either Total Knowledge or come across a truly immutable Absolute should not make us regard our rational endeavors as a futile exercise. Rebelling against that unavoidable and totally reasonable deterministic conclusion human beings maintain that life-giving movement alive. The interaction between our eternal **hopefulness** together with our also eternal **hopelessness** provided the spark that ignited the creative motion in *our universe*.

In that ever-present flux, our mental system, and its tools, for understanding the universe would appear to freeze that movement, losing in that same process the essence of it: the flowing itself. It would be, in a way, similar to the method of desiccating the universe in order to *preserve it*, (to avoid changes and decay) and make it fit for *human consumption*. Whatever the object of the reasoning process may be, it is clear that an indefinite part of its vital flow will inevitably be dried out as much as possible, and then the object will be preserved. Then human beings will feed on it for as long as it is rationally edible. Naturally enough **eternal preservation is unattainable**. Rational food is perishable stuff. *Science being a most eloquent example of it*. The paradoxical thing, that adds a touch of irony to it, would appear to be that **the date** on which its fitness for consumption **expires** can never be decided in advance, but it would appear to be forced upon reason by the universe itself, as it decides to show that what seemed to be immobile (dead) has been made to look perceptibly mobile (alive).

From a more dramatic viewpoint we could also argue along similar lines and say that if we were to take reason and logic as implements which would be somewhat solidifying the universe as they tried to make sense of it, they could be charged with the count of halting its vital flows, and with being to some degree hostile factors in the universal environment. And at this juncture we might wonder if we could really have been found **guilty on that count** and condemned to live a life of tribulations stemming from our rationality, as the Christian faith would seem to indicate with its "*Vale of tears*" image.

How befitting and beautiful it would be if those tears shed from our eyes were the sublimation of those vital flows of the universe which our *reason had been incapable of incorporating* into its understanding. If that were to be the case we could say that every time we feel some pain or suffering that our thinking cannot explain away, **the tears** that well up in our eyes would be the "**pearls of reason**", of our precious, but also limited and somewhat powerless reason. To the extent that our understanding may increase, by means of a rationality able to perceive and incorporate those vital universal flows into its processes, those pearls of reason will tend to become less and less abundant.

In the clash between reason and the Universe **movement always prevails**. All our rational structures will eventually be razed to the ground because they are always built on the wrong basis, however slightly that may be. And what makes it intriguing is that there are no right hypotheses at all. Unless, of course, we have reached that divine status and achieved Total Knowledge. And here perhaps we might wonder whether it would be desirable for rational beings to obtain that. We have seen how bored and stressed we can get in these times of confinement, when our rational mind is being deprived of a healthy intake of varying perceptions, would we want to experience what it feels like to be deprived of any movement at all?. Would we want to live in that seemingly inescapable horrendous and unchangeable eternity?.. There seems to be an inherent impossibility for a reasoning being to be able to envisage what it would feel like to be divine. The human mind, based on the perception of changes, would have to give up its essential nature to become a God-like entity.

Temporality vs Eternity. Could there be a path, or a point in space, that would allow them both to transform into one another?. We have argued not. Infinity would take care of that by exacting that endless bridges be crossed forever.

And yet our human mind **cannot subtract itself** from wanting to obtain omniscience. Consequently the only way for a reasoner to behave would be that of having to push back endlessly the frontiers that surround their particular world. And it might be regarded as reasonable to believe that whenever a man died in a *rational manner*, fighting back the protective and yet enslaving influence of the Absolute, his blood would add a little more self-awareness to the universe, and what better purpose for human reason could be wished than to contribute towards the realization of that **eternal longing for immobility** that runs through the Universe?. It could be said that from this standpoint our reason would, then, be in harmony with that universal **Desire**.

The nature of Language.

In our first escapade into infinity with my special guide Achilles, I remember him telling me about the **inadequacy** of language to capture the full nature of the universe. The way he summarized it was quite enlightening to me: "**Language** vs **Infinity**, the never-ending struggle between a **bounding** implement and a **boundless** concept".

By the time our trip had finished he had helped me to visualize the basic forces permeating the universe and our human existence. He identified eternal movement as the overriding force in nature and he also explained to me how our rational mind went about making sense of what it perceived. But we didn't talk much about the nature of language though. That did not worry me much, however, for both times that he had waved goodbye to me he had made sure that I remained aware of his foremost advice by pointing to his laurels, thus reminding me of how sensible the **idealist perspective** was.

I also believed that it would make sense to think that the development of language would have followed the same pattern as the acquisition of knowledge, that is to say the design of ever enlarging concentric circles. As with the origins of life, those initial sounds, that could be regarded as a reasonable code to pass information of our surroundings, may very well lie concealed somewhere within the naturally inaccurate rational processes that we carry out to understand the movements of the universe.

For the sake of a reasonable account let us suppose that there was a "*first instance*". Within the closest circles of our environment this first set of few sounds, -- that had codified some observations useful for our survival,-- together with the awareness of its usefulness, set in motion the development of language. First in its oral expression naturally, and adapting and evolving as we spread round the world. Then there came the need to make those useful perceptions a little more **durable** than just sounds so we started drawing and engraving the images of our world. Along, then, came the pictographs, and the petroglyphs, which not only gave our perceptions the property of more lastingness but could also be used as **teaching** tools. Later on we invented the hieroglyphs and the ideograms with which we were able to portray more complex ideas. Around the same time we also discovered some lighter, more flexible, and manageable material to reproduce our knowledge on, and that made possible some budding cultural expansion and interchange. And so on. Nowadays, after a few thousand years we have developed a much more sophisticated set of linguistic tools that allow us to codify the world we perceive in a way that bears little resemblance with that of our early ancestors.

When we talked about the process of acquiring knowledge we pointed towards the fact that it is done by identifying any new particular change observed in our little universe, be it in terms of objects, feelings, actions or any other category. This identification always comes about through the act of comparison against our previous understanding and by careful analysis discovering differences and similarities. All these activities are carried out using language labels already at our disposal; with the necessary nuances added to the labels to include the new finding, or if need be creating a new name for it.

And much in the same manner as we know who we are by contrasting our movements to others', words also *"find"* their meaning when around others. All words within a language try to capture that small nuance that others do not quite reflect. That's the reason why we have to create new ones when we observe something not previously known. This naturally means that as we expand our awareness our vocabulary also expands. Not always necessarily creating new words, sometimes just mixing, or modifying slightly, the ones we already have.

We find it impossible to dissociate rational thinking from language. We have said that thinking is based upon the perception of movement, and the only way to reason through it is by *sticking labels* to those movements and combining them in a way that will make some sort of logical sense, however temporary though that may be. On the other hand if by any chance we wanted to experience some kind of rationally meaningless language we could just try and repeat the same word an indefinitely large number of times. We might realise then how our reasoning mind would start losing its bearings and begin a different process of getting into contact with its surroundings. In some religions they practise this technique to enter a different dimension of consciousness, hoping perhaps to unite with a timeless divinity. Same word over and over again. An unchanging way of reaching a timeless and static ecstasy.

But unlike that monotonous and monochromatic path towards the **One** used by some, the reasoners choose a dynamic and polychromatic route towards expressing their particular knowledge of the world. And it is along this road that they may realize that having a good command of their language will provide them with better brushes and a more colorful palette with which to illustrate the vision of their universe, and be able **to share** it with others, thus fulfilling one of the most **basic needs** of men: the need to feel that what they perceive amounts to a **reality** possibly **common** for them all.

To represent our world, language has become the best instrument at our disposal, and its mastery will increase the probabilities of making our descriptions much more readily accessible to others. But in the same way that our world is a construct of our mind, slightly different for each of us, the **content** of language, what it symbolizes, **will vary also** to some degree from mind to mind. So when a conversation takes place a speaker may expose a series of words, of snapshots, which in his mind are imbued with the movements he perceived at the time of his experience, whereas the listeners would imbue those same words with their particular representations.[8] To summarize this concept we could say that each of us breathes our own life into the language we use, which of necessity will always be similar, and different, to a certain extent. And despite that inevitable differences we shall carry on verbalizing the view of our universe in **the hope of seeing** a semblance of its replication in the eyes of another rational being. That **semblance of likeness**, which implies a certain level of **understanding**, and also of sharing a somewhat common reality, is what all human beings always long for.

Overcoming singularity is an overwhelming need. At its most basic nature will always try to **replicate itself**, given the adequate conditions, to stop sensing the anxiety of eternal movement. Self-replication, by nullifying movement, would confer a sense of security stemming from the knowledge of being surrounded by alike entities. It would appear that **distinctness**, -- infinite movements,-- is something that causes a degree of anxiety within

---

8   We could imagine words as little transparent crystal boxes into which we pour the content of our life experiences. While acting as listeners we do not let the other people have access to the boxes contents, but the moment we take up the role of speakers people have the possibility, and sometimes the capacity, of being able to glimpse that what fills our linguistics crystal boxes has much more to do with what we are than with the "reality" we may be trying to portray. In other words, the language we use, together with **how** we use it, says normally as much, if not more, about ourselves than it does about whatever we may be attempting to describe.

the universe. This anxiety would force all the particular beings to encounter some degree of commonality. And given the inherent constant change in the universe those particular beings, whatever they may be, will have to keep on reproducing themselves to create as similar surroundings as possible. The degree of that similarity would also depend on the essence of the other particular forces at play which at the same time will strive to avoid as much friction as possible. Everything involved in a never ending **process of infinite understanding**. By understanding something **that** something becomes **part of ourselves** and it is no longer perceived as being different and as a consequence we increase our consciousness. It is difficult to overstate the essential role of language in our endeavors to quell the anxiety that derives from seeing ourselves as singularities.

Another important language worth mentioning here would be mathematics. This language is undoubtedly the most precise we have invented to represent the dynamics of the universe. But despite its possibilities to capture images far beyond our physical capabilities, using infinitesimal calculus, both in integration and differentiation, it will never be able to portray a perfectly accurate picture of the world's forces at play. These ever changing forces will make the apparently **solid shapes** of numbers pale into **amorphous** unrecognizable values. The useful natural numbers we manage for our daily operations all carry a **secret expiry date**, inaccessible to us, but that is unveiled at the right time by the universe itself.

In pursuit of happiness

Right at this point, we don't really know what happiness is, what it consists of, or what it depends upon. And given that state of ignorance we are in we could very well start by asking ourselves some questions about it. For instance, where would we locate the possible seat of our happiness?. And, then, how could we visualize a likely path to follow in order to get there, if there were any?.

In keeping with our overall view about where our reality lies, the answer to the first question can only be that it is also in our mind where the seeds of all our feelings reside. And it would not be considered **ethical**, or **aesthetic**, enough for the forces of creation to have placed them in a kind of unsymmetrical location, favoring some privileged individuals more than their fellow humans. We believe that the universe has given us all the **same possibilities** to attain that feeling of happiness. And it is **within ourselves**. So we don't need to start running after some kind of material object lying somewhere outside our sphere of influence. The key is to strike a balance between what we are, at a certain point, and our own personal and inevitable process of development.

Looking at it from a material perspective it might also be worth considering to what extent our achievements should keep within a sensible grasp not to upset unduly the worlds of those that we may have to come across in order to get them. This would be ethically acceptable and would also make for a better social environment. Ethically acceptable, because there are times when parading our *"achievements"* in front of those who have not had the possibility of attaining them may not be ethically endorsed.

Without mentioning, of course, that it would be deleterious to our social environment for the negative feelings it would arouse, eventually reaching back to those who motivated such feelings. In other words, our behaviour would not be questionable at all if whatever we had, which appeared in principle as somewhat desirable, could have been had by everybody else. The only thing preventing that from happening being their own **particular idiosyncrasies**. This would mean they would have followed their own **naturally distinct** tendencies and would not feel aggrieved by the differences. Differences, once they are understood and are incorporated into ourselves are no longer perceived as such. They cease to show that facet that made them something unsettling.

We know how far we are from that type of world, but that should not dissuade us from working towards creating that kind of social environment where our material differences, or possessions, would literally not upset any member of the community, because we all could have had them had we wanted to. In the meantime on a personal level we should all be more careful about vaunting our "**assets**" in front of those who might feel hurt or discriminated against by what we do. And by assets we mean not just material things, but also the excessive pride and haughtiness that comes from misusing little bits of knowledge.

Then we have some physiological contributors to the overall feeling of happiness. In this context the adequate covering of the most basic needs of our species such as food, warmth, shelter, sex, and so on, also provides a fundamental platform from which to reach other levels of happiness. Without it the psychological and spiritual levels of happiness fade away into non-existence.

It might be worth noting that on a psychological plane, and thinking of men as social beings, some degree of happiness for men does depend on their being recognised, within their society, as individuals with their own useful value. The **recognition of their own usefulness** is essential to develop their self-esteem and their sense of belonging to a greater whole. And as we have seen so often by now, to feel well balanced we need to cover **the two natural tendencies** in our mind, the one that asserts our uniqueness and also the one that allows us to sense we are not alone. From this social perspective it is also interesting to notice that what we call material development **may not play any significant role** in the relative happiness of the members of a society as such. We believe that those men who lived in early civilizations, in prehistoric tribes, had as much a chance to achieve that degree of social happiness as we have nowadays. The only requisite was to be recognized as useful individuals, and **not be discriminated against**, that's to say being treated as equals to most people. Those needs are as relevant today as they have always been. This idea would be in keeping with the notion of there being some kind of an eternally balanced universal justice, which would allow all beings in history to reach happiness by finding the right **equilibrium within their environment**.

That was on a socio-psychological plane. Assuming that those conditions of individual recognition take place in their due measure, there is another way to access real happiness, but this occurs on an intellectual plane and it is naturally confined within the mind of every individual. It has to do with our way of acquiring rational knowledge. Every time we solve a minor issue in our particular world, and make it fit into that monistic knowledge lying at the base of our bubble-ship, which is what makes us what we are, we reach a new level of understanding. It is this transient level of **understanding** what translates into a feeling as close to happiness as we can possibly get. **Comprehension** dissolves discomfort while miscomprehension magnifies it. The trouble is it is not given to us, but rather we have to **work rationally** for it. So for those reasoning individuals it would be like reaching "*heavens*", metaphorically speaking, by climbing up a staircase made up of infinite steps. And the beauty of it would be that those steps would not be laid there in front of them, but they would have to **carve them** out of the universe's stuff and then **assemble them themselves too!.**

I will allow myself to express the idea again, hopefully to help clarify how the workings of our mind can provide us with a key to opening the door to true happiness. The key is provided at the end of every mental processing that takes place in our mind. At the point when we sense that that little unknown thing that has come into our space has been properly understood and placed within that all-embracing monistic view of the universe. It is in that satisfying feeling of understanding, to accommodate a new perception and **give birth** to a new and **wiser self**, where we should find the key to **the gate** of that extraordinary place where real happiness can be found. Extraordinary place, and yet accessible to all of us. **Understanding is the path** to follow to transcend ourselves, to communicate with the Cosmos and eventually experience that elating feeling of Oneness human kind is always longing for. Every time that we transcend ourselves we savour the **greatest taste** of happiness men can feel. And thanks to our ever-changing universe the scope for exercising our understanding and feeling real happiness will never be exhausted.

We believe that there are *other paths* that lead to that state of ecstatic happiness experienced by many **Mystics** of different religions, when they talk about a feeling of spiritual union with the supreme forces of their beliefs. That feeling of spiritual union does not take place on a rational level and it might possibly be more difficult to visualise and engage. If we may employ an analogy used previously our reasoning process would be trying to access heavens climbing up a staircase made up of infinite steps, crafted with rational sweat and pain, whereas the Mystics would enjoy the privilege of a *"supersonic"* lift, whose location would also be in a place with unknown geographical coordinates.

Some sociological features in an ever-changing universe.

It stands to reason that all aspects of our social interactions are going to bear the cachet of the workings of our mind. Our relationships will be subjected to the characteristic properties of our rational process common to most of us. As we have already seen what will differ will be mainly the data that we manage in that process. That data will be to some extent common and to some degree particular to every individual. **Upon the common data social reality will be built** and become the main market in our social transactions. The particular reality of each of us will remain unrecognized as tradable items unless, through some scientific feat, we turn it visible to those who govern the main market and they approve of it. It appears logical that most, if not all, of our social exchanges can only take place within the established common reality. Here we can readily swap and share feelings, emotions, activities, and so on. So the question would arise as to why there are times when, while practising some human interactions within our common reality, tense or violent situations come to the fore. We think that this has a lot to do with the **pendular momentum** that is always taking place in our mind.

Let us assume for the purpose of this analysis that two old friends meet in the street. They both seem to find the situation very pleasurable and they start to converse. As time passes, no surprisingly, the pleasure gradually diminishes. But the crux of the matter is that it doesn't do it **at the same pace** for both of them. The differences in their own particular world, will exert a definite influence on how they perceive the development of the encounter. Imagine that one has just come out from a longish period spent closed in within his known world, where nothing much rationally stimulating was happening. The pendular momentum in his mind would be moving **towards the particular end** in search of some novelty with which to feed his rational needs. And then the other has just happened to be going home after a night of revelry at a party, longing for a rest within what symbolized the apparent stability of his world: his own room. Who do we think would be the first to start feeling that what began as a **pleasurable** circumstance was turning into a bit of an **irritation?**.

It would appear that the one who had just bumped into his friend when going home after a party, wishing to allow his senses to have a respite, would be the first to reach what we call the "**saturation point**", beyond which any kind of pleasure starts turning into displeasure. The need to reinforce his identity through contrasting himself to others would be non-existent. He had probably had more than enough self-reinforcement at the party. But in his friend that need is still overwhelming. As the conversation carries on the one who was going home starts to feel a little annoyance creeping into his mind. He begins looking for a reasonable excuse to disengage from the conversation, hopefully without unnecessarily hurting his friend. On the other hand the one who is still extracting pleasure from the conversation, because his mind was in the mode to feed from particular factors, does his best to **prolong the gratification**. Now we only have to stretch the situation a bit more in time to visualize the strain being built up and a potential point of conflict.

Not only is it convenient to develop techniques to know how and when to disengage during our social interactions, but also, and more important, it is to be aware that these **asymmetric situations** are going to be a constant feature in our life owing to that ever-present movement that defines the universe, life as a whole, and our social interchanges in particular. We, all, will reach that "*saturation point*" at one moment or another. But unfortunately we will never do it in a synchronous manner. This means that there will always be someone less satisfied. Someone that would have preferred it to carry on a little further. And this is the **thin edge of the wedge towards feelings of frustration**.

In this respect, given that our elemental mind is conditioned to satisfy itself to its maximum extent, that is to say until it reaches its saturation point, where things start slowly turning into their **opposites**,[9] it would be advisable for humans to take a leaf of the Stoics' philosophy book and learn to develop a little self-control. If we managed to act according to the principle of: "*Stop before getting to the saturation point*", our mind would never feel satiated and would retain a good memory of that experience. We would always be wanting to come back to that person, or to that activity. Within this approach there is not much difference between our connections with people and our relation to food or drinks. However appealing it may be, leave yourself always with the feeling that you could have had a bit more, that you are not entirely full. You will remain with a good taste and your mind will not wince at the thought of it again. But, of course, it is not easy. Our mind requires the appropriate ecosystem and time to develop the needed energy and insight to help us refrain from exhausting a source of pleasure. But we can all learn. It is within our power. Time we all have . The right ecosystem, education and opportunities, is what is needed.

---

9   Who hasn't seen, or personally experienced, that in some relationships those character traits that seemed so appealing at the beginning have turned into unattractive ones, because of excessive exposure, or having reached, and gone past, the saturation point?. Have we been designed to always exhaust whatever it is that we derive pleasure from?. Some would argue for that to be the case. But what I would find most illuminating about this situation is the inherent underlying lesson about the relative nature of reality. It is quite a clear illustration of how it is dependent upon our state of mind, that is to say something can be a source of both, pleasure or pain, determined by how it is perceived.

It might be worth exploring a bit further the enormous implications of the fact that our mind seems to have an **unstoppable** and **built-in** desire to squeeze to the last drop every source of pleasure it discovers. Be it in personal relationships, or in working activities Every time that our reasoning process puts some scientific order into some studied particulars, -- which is a source of pleasure in itself --, and comes up with some useful applications for the knowledge acquired, the chances are that those applications will run the full course of their usefulness up to their saturation point, **... and unfortunately beyond**.

We only have to look at the state of the planet nowadays to realize how capable we are of turning great inventions, or discoveries, into problems because of that inbuilt trait of our mind.. Let us just quote three of the most prominent and current concerns: the enormous generation of plastic waste invading all ecosystems, the increase of CO_2 in the atmosphere due to the excessive use of carbon fossil fuels, and the immense detrimental effects on habitats by mass tourism, often done under the pretense of the right to knowledge. Something which did start as a pursuit of that natural thirst for greater awareness was gradually turned into a mainly deleterious activity. Curiously enough that point, at which we realize that what was, once, a very fruitful answer has turned into a definite problem, seems to be **the boundary** to a new state of greater level of consciousness. And it is here that some questions seem to loom large: Do we **always** have to reach that tipping point?. Will we ever learn how our primeval mind works, and its basic nature ?. And if we do, will we be able to do something about it, or, suffer the consequences of our **rational shortsightedness** over and over again?.

Another sociological field of human tension that has come to the fore prominently in the last few decades, and that has been magnified noticeably by the current state of confinement is that experienced by couples. The present state of affairs has inevitably led to a marked increase in *domestic violence*. The situation with couples living together, under the same roof, is in a way similar to the one portrayed at the beginning of this chapter about two friends happily bumping into each other in the street, but reaching the moment of disengagement experiencing rather different feelings. One having reached his saturation point, the other being left somewhat unfulfilled.

From a psychological point of view the situation between a couple will not differ. Each person will have their own pendular momentum going up and down their cone-shaped minds, moving to and fro, from their particular world to the universal. They will always cross each other at one point and feel for a time that some pleasurable interaction is being done. They might even find themselves sometimes moving in the same direction, which would give them a little more scope to enjoy a longer pleasurable interaction. But unfortunately, or rather by the nature of things, whether our paths cross, or go in the same direction for a little more time, the fact remains that we all have different speeds of movement, and this will mean that there will always be someone that will feel let down when the natural disengagement comes. In the case of a couple this is made much worse by the fact that they **can't escape** from their source of disappointment or frustration. And, within a small space, that can only snowball.

Living together is one of the most difficult endeavors human beings can undertake. We are handicapped by the workings of our rational processes. We enter into relationships gauging people by our own principles, looking for partners who can share most of our values --(*nature performing its self-replication law through our reasoning mind*)--, which inevitably creates the consequent expectations of wanting to be repaid with the same kind and the same value. I fear those expectations are doomed. (*And only non-*

rational, or divine, entities can endure not having expectations!).
The closest humans could get to a repayment would be to one of
"similar kind and similar value" and, as we know, that is an open
gate for very contrasting interpretations. To sum it up, in a world
in constant change **THERE ARE NO PARALLEL LINES**. Any
structure, social or otherwise, that tries to depict that concept
without making allowances for that eternal movement is bound
to **feel cracks** appearing sooner or later, most likely leading to a
complete collapse.

Separation, or divorce, is the natural response to a relationship
that does not fulfill the required psychological needs of either
partner. Self awareness is essential. Immediately after that comes
the need to be recognised. As regards self awareness it is most
important to have a reasonably wide circle of people to relate
with. Let us remember that through comparing and contrasting
ourselves with others is how we discover who we are. A **balanced
social habitat** will make for a **balanced person**. On the other
hand a person who depends **almost exclusively on the other
partner** for self awareness will end up inevitably antagonizing
them through the quasi-constant negation, or questioning, of
their opinions, *something which* **we need to do** *in an instinctive
way* **to find out who we are**. The trouble here, of course, is that
the target of our opposing actions is just only one person, and
that will very rapidly wear away the layers of endurance and will
eventually cause a great deal of irritation. And if that activity of
questioning every aspect of our partner's expressions is coupled
with the possibility that what they might be needing is precisely
the opposite, that is to say reinforcement of themselves through
the **sharing of a common reality**, we end up with a most
explosive mixture of feelings, and predictable results.

Apart from that toxic environment, where some degree of conflict
will always come to the surface, *individual recognition in this type*

of contexts, where either of the members, or both, depend mainly on each other for their **psychological well-being**, will always end up suffering from severe **undernourishment**, resulting in depressive states. In those relatively healthy relationships though, where that vital requirement of being recognised is reasonably fulfilled, we could progressively aim towards achieving an equal footing within the relationship, sensing also the extent to which we were valued for our contribution. Let us remind ourselves here that **being useful** is another very important requirement that **needs to be satisfied** in the human species's psyche.

We could also have a look at some sociological aspects that take place in our interactions. As we have realized by now, one of the vital needs in men, as social entities, is that of being able **to feel that we are not alone**, that our view is shared by those around us. In pursuit of that underlying feeling of oneness, we sometimes impose our reality in a very disagreeable manner upon those unfortunate people around us, bombarding them "*generously*" with our wonderful music for example, or any other similarly intrusive activity. Other times, in a more polite manner we request other people's attention to the things we see, hear, or do, compelled to share our perceptions, and longing to find out if what they perceive is the same as what we perceive. There is a definite sense of relief if they agree to do what they are asked. Relief that would turn into elation if, after that, there happened to be some *concurrence of opinion* about the nature of the object in question.

Naturally enough there is nothing much to worry about in our social interchanges when there is an apparent agreement about our reality. Frictions start appearing the moment that bit of common reality is being subjected to the influence of our own particular area of reality, inevitably coloring it with a slightly different hue. This, which might be **disturbing** to those people who conceive reality as something that can stand on its own outside the observer, would be a completely **natural** conclusion to those who believe nature is affected by how we perceive it. Therefore in a sociological context the former, those who believe reality is independent of them, will tend to get **more upset** if opposed, and argue **most fiercely** to make everybody conform to their vision of it. Whereas the Idealists, those who believe reality to be a construct of the mind, will take their differences **in their stride** and not be bothered by something that is, of necessity, an obvious conclusion. In this sense Idealism makes also for a much **better sociological environment** in which to express ourselves.

Regarding the subject of expressions, there are, in some romance languages at least, linguistic clichés which do not work in favor of a better habitat for social interaction. The Spanish *"no tienes razón"*, the French *"tu n'as pas raison"*, the Italian *"non hai ragione"*, are all phrases that do smack of a certain disdain for the other people's views and do not benefit the flow of the conversation because of their *antagonizing effect*. Apart from the fact that they **are not correct** since we assume that the rational process is something common to our species and that the only thing that varies is the data that it handles. Therefore if we want people to change their opinions we have to allow them to perceive the bits of information missing from their processes.--(Here is when having a decent mastery of our language helps to put across that bit of information we want the other person to understand and incorporate). That way they will inevitably arrive at a view which will be similar enough to ours so as to be considered the same. Let us remember, here, once more that **"total equality"** is an inconceivable concept in our incessant universe. So, in our social interactions, different views, or opinions, should be expected as a matter of course. They are a natural consequence of how each individual sees the world from their particular perspective, and as such they should be respected and not looked down upon in any way, *even when not shared in the slightest degree*. If we were able to live up to this idea of embracing differences as something **naturally unavoidable** a great deal of social tension and conflict would be reduced. We could also go as far as to say that apart from being inevitable they are also **essential agents** in our own personal development.

Also from a linguistic perspective we could try to understand some possible character traits of human beings and the pendular momentum of their mind as portrayed by the way we use language. We have for instance people whose language is mainly made up of a **concatenation of clichés**, seemingly using the same commonplaces, machine-gunned quite happily and with *"complete certainty"*, to describe what they might regard as identical situations, (*the reasoning processes of these people while doing that would be at a minimum*) , or those whose **harmonious and calm** way of delivery recreates the image of some artists trying to depict a new facet of reality, with the linguistic palette at their disposal, always giving the impression that somehow they **cannot quite capture it**. Although we, as observers, might be impressed and moved by the pathos emanating from their efforts. (*With their rational powers probably working at their maximum*). And also those, whose high tone of voice, while socializing in normal gatherings, denotes as much their need **to impose their vision** on others, aiming to replicate themselves,   as their **insecurity and fear** about their being *"alone"*. Not to mention the mental turmoil that it nearly always reflects. Although regarding the latter it could also be argued that most of the talking we do usually **helps to exorcise** our little demons, and by objectivizing them in our conversations it plays a major role in the increase of our understanding. From this perspective the social value of talking as regards our mental well being **cannot be overestimated**.

On a collective level as well, all throughout human History, we have sought to replicate ourselves by imposing, **not freely exchanging**, our little absolutes, our values, and our principles while invading and colonizing other societies under the guise of advancing civilization. That, I believe, is much more a reflection of our own frailties and weaknesses than a generous philanthropic endeavor. Of course we will feel a greater sense of safety and security as we create replicas of ourselves, but at a cost of not respecting the natural right of other peoples to express themselves as they are. We have to learn **to live in tune with those differences** that, in normal conditions, not only do they not pose a threat to us but also enrich our rational processes and our human existence. The present trend of quasi unrestrained globalization seems to be running *counter to the rhythms* of the natural processes. This unparalleled homogenization of men may place much of **the species' diversity** at risk. And were that loss to occur we would be much the poorer for it. These are times **to slow down**, and learn again to move **in harmony with the flows of mother Nature.**

Author's Biography

Pedro Camarero Prieto (Burgos 1948) started developing his interest in language and thought in London, the city to which he moved in 1972. In 1978 he studied a Degree in Modern Languages at what is now known as the University of Westminster. After two years in Italy he returned to London to do a Masters in Romance Languages and Literature, at King's College, specializing in Jorge Luis Borges. His dissertation entitled "An approach to the concept of infinity in the stories of J.L. Borges" received abundant praise from the Board of Professors, who highly recommended its publication. This booklet is but a brief account of some of the thoughts of the philosophical framework carved out of the reading and ensuing reflection upon Borges's writings while trying to decipher his universe.

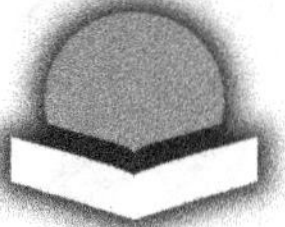

www.ingramcontent.com/pod-product-compliance
Lightning Source LLC
Chambersburg PA
CBHW081406130726
47998CB00011B/3086